SHAKY HANDS

A Kid's Guide to Parkinson's Disease

SOANIA MATHUR BSC, MD, CCFP

CONTRIBUTIONS BY SARIKA, NEHA AND MEERAYA MATHUR

This book is dedicated to my loving husband Arun without whose support and encouragement this book or any of my other accomplishments would not have been possible. You are my rock. And also to our three beautiful daughters—Sarika, Neha and Meeraya. You give me strength when I feel weak and give me reason to persevere when the obstacles seem insurmountable. Your enduring optimism buoys my own. You have shown me the good that can come from a life-changing diagnosis like Parkinson's—that empathy and compassion can be born from adversity. Thank you my darlings for holding my shaky hands as we face this journey together…

Introduction

You probably had never heard of Parkinson's until someone you love told you that they have it. Maybe you noticed that something was going on—that they seemed different. But you probably weren't sure what it was, or why things were changing.

Were you worried that something really bad was happening? You're not alone. There are many other kids, all around the world, feeling the same way.

Parkinson's disease (PD) affects the brain, which controls the body. When you have Parkinson's, you can't control the way your body moves like you could before. Parkinson's affects one in a hundred people over the age of 60, but can also be found in younger people. There isn't a cure yet, but scientists are working very hard to find one.

We don't know why most of the people who get Parkinson's do. But just because someone in your family has it, doesn't mean you will too. In fact chances are, you won't!

It is only natural to be scared of something when you don't know anything about it. I am a doctor and a mom and I have Parkinson's, so I decided to write this book to help you understand. Throughout, you will also find special sidebars, all written from a kid's point of view—kids who happen to be my daughters: Neha, age 10, and Sarika, age 13 plus a special message from my youngest, Meeraya. Who better than kids who've grown up with a "shaky Mom" to let you know how they feel?

It is my big wish that after reading these pages, any fear that you are feeling is replaced by understanding and hope.

Table of Contents

3
Why do you shake?

13
So how do you feel?

23
But doesn't your medicine make you feel better?

29
You're still the one I love

39
I can make a difference!

People with Parkinson's are inspiring,
They are many people worth admiring.
Many are affected,
And many still undetected.
Many scientists are trying to find a cure,
These are the people with a soul so pure,
That what you see is love,
That is sent from above.
Some people have a tremor,
Other people can't remember.
Parkinson's looks scary,
But most people who have it are very merry.
These people have suffered enough,
And they have been very tough.
They should all be known for what they have gone through,
I hope you know that too.
My heroes they are,
For them I'd go far.
When the cure has been found,
The disease will not be around.
When that day arrives,
It will change lives.

—Neha

1

WHY DO YOU SHAKE?

"I see your hands shake a bit in the morning and sometimes you have a hard time walking... why does that happen to you?"

The short answer to that question is this: Some people shake because they have Parkinson's disease. But I know you want the long answer because you want to know **why** Parkinson's makes certain people shake, right? Well, believe it or not, it all starts with the brain—one of the most important parts of your body. In fact, you can't live without it! The brain is the big boss and it controls everything—your eyesight, your hearing, your thinking, your breathing, your memory, your movement—essentially, you! But how does something in your head control your fingers or toes? They're pretty far from your brain.

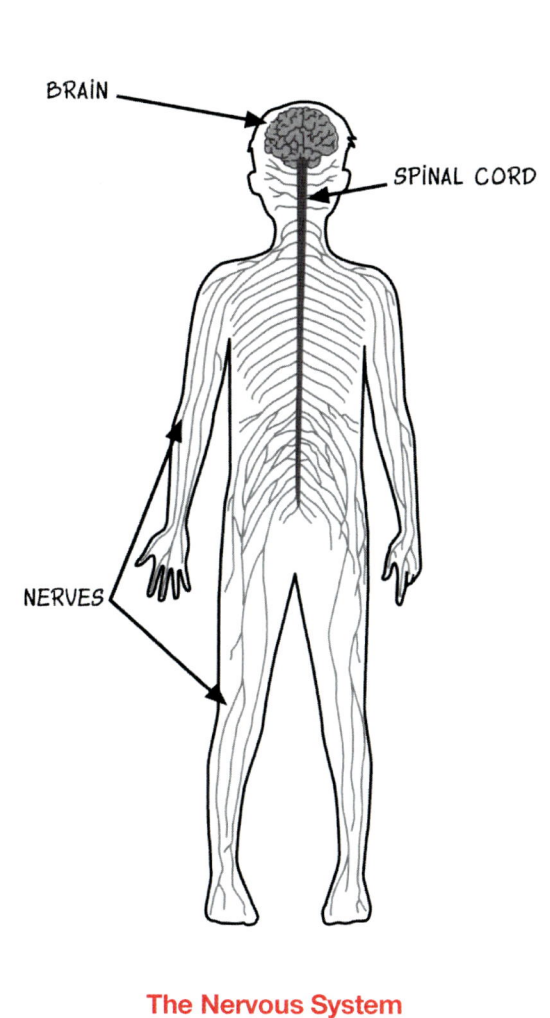

The Nervous System

That's the magic performed by the nervous system, the enormous network of nerves throughout the body. Nerve cells like long, thin wires make up this system. Bundled together, they carry information back and forth from the brain out to different parts of the body and information from the body back to the brain. But every boss needs helpers to do a good job. The nerves and the spinal cord (a bundle of nerves that are protected by your

> **INFO BOX**
>
> Every living thing is made up of building blocks called cells and your body is made up of almost 100 trillion of them (that's more than 14 thousand times the number of people living in the whole world!). Cells are very tiny—you really can't see them without a microscope. There are hundreds of different kinds, such as skin cells, muscle cells, brain cells, all responsible for doing different things that you need to live and stay healthy. Some cells are responsible for carrying oxygen to parts of your body (blood cells), while others help to digest your food (stomach cells). The cells in your brain are called **neurons** (nyur-ons). The neurons have long projections or tails called axons. And a bunch of these axons is what makes up a nerve. These neurons and nerves are responsible for sending messages around your brain and then out to your body to allow you to walk, for example, or chew your food, or to breathe. The way they talk to each other is with chemical messengers called **"neurotransmitters"** (nyur-o-tranz-mitters) and dopamine is a type of neurotransmitter.

vertebrae or back bone). work hard to make sure that whatever the boss wants gets done, pronto!

So how do the brain's instructions get from one place to another? By a cool system of chemical messengers (called neurotransmitters) and electrical impulses. Say you decide that you want to move your hand. Just like the Big Boss in his upstairs office, **the brain sends out a memo**—a chemical messenger. The boss selects the right messenger for the job and off the messenger goes to find the right neuron, where it makes a tiny electrical signal. This signal travels down the "wire" of the neuron until it gets to the end. Then, the next neuron sends out another neurotransmitter that travels to another neuron, triggering it to send the next electrical signal down that neuron. This happens over and over until the information gets to wherever the boss said it should end up. It's kind of like a relay race or a row of dominoes when you've pushed one and then the next one

pushes the one next to it and so on and so on. Eventually the message gets from your brain to your hand.

Now what? Well, each nerve controls a muscle. And each muscle makes your hand move a certain way. Many muscles have to work together to make your hand move the way your brain wants it to. You may be saying to yourself "But I don't think about it, I just move my hand!" And you do just move, but its only possible because your brain gave your nerves the master plan. So all you have to do is think "I want to eat that apple." It's your brain that has to do all the figuring out of how to make one muscle do this and another one do that so that you can pick up that apple and take a big bite. And it's a good thing too. You might get pretty hungry if you had to figure it all out yourself!

It's a pretty complicated setup. Millions of nerves, many different types of neurotransmitters and they all have to work together to get your body to move smoothly. Each of these messengers plays an important role. One might signal a muscle to tense up, while another may tell it to relax. All the instructions are necessary to move in a normal way.

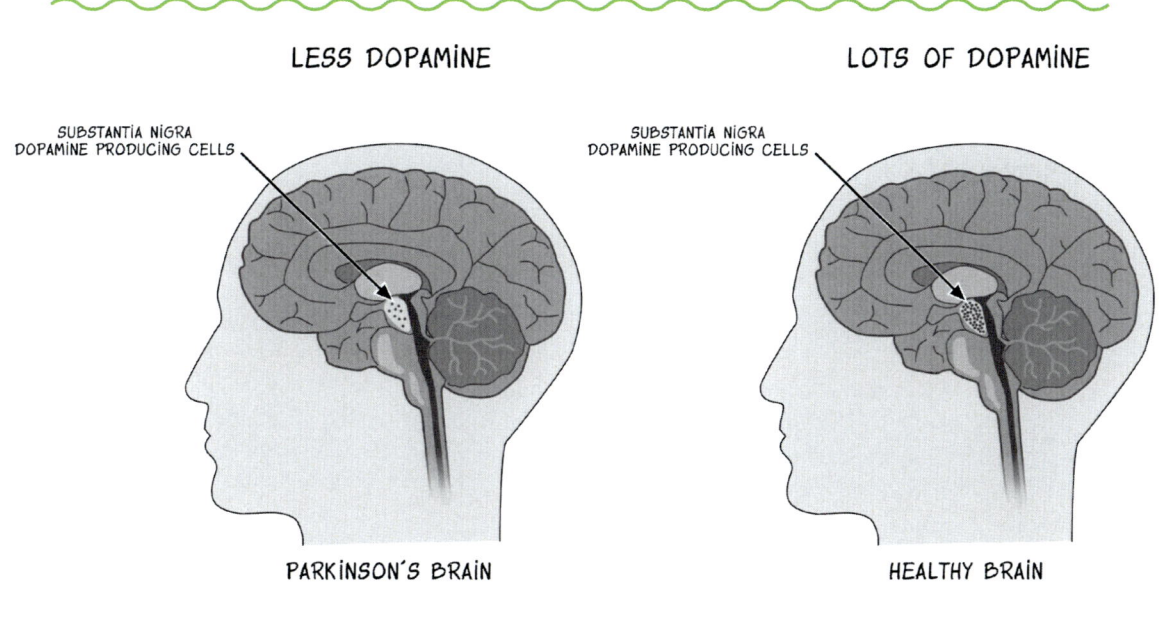

So here's what is happening in the brain of somebody who has Parkinson's. Maybe you've already guessed that it has something to do with the messengers. And you're right. One of the problems is in a small section of the brain called the **Substantia Nigra** (sub-stan-sha nie-gra). There are special cells there that make something called **dopamine** (doe-pa-meen). Dopamine is one of the messengers that helps your muscles move properly.

The brain of a person with Parkinson's disease doesn't make enough dopamine because the cells that are supposed to make it slowly die. Doctors and researchers don't know exactly why, but when about 60% to 70% of the cells aren't there to do their job anymore, movement starts to be a problem. **Without enough dopamine,** the muscles become confused. They begin to shake (called tremor) or they may get stiff. The body just doesn't move the way it should and the person ends up with the symptoms of Parkinson's.

Sarika Says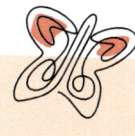

"The way Parkinson's works may be a little difficult to understand. Just think about it like this. Your bike needs oil the same way your muscles need dopamine. Without oil, the gears on your bike may get a little stiff and the bike may not move as well as it used to. Same thing for your muscles. At least that's how I think of it."

2

SO HOW DO YOU FEEL?

"Why doesn't Grandpa smile as much anymore?"

"Why can't you stop your hand from shaking?"

So now you know that in Parkinson's disease, the body doesn't always get the right signals from the brain. What difference does that make? A whole lot! Without the right instructions going from our brain to our body, we can't move normally. Our bodies just don't work the way they should.

How do doctors know if someone has Parkinson's? It's not a simple puzzle to figure out because right now there is no real tool, blood test, or special x-ray that doctors can use to tell them if someone has this disease. Instead doctors count on what patients complain about (**symptoms**) and what they see during their check up (**signs**). Then they use these symptoms and signs to figure out whether someone has Parkinson's disease or something else. So what exactly do those with Parkinson's complain about or mention to their doctor?

> **INFO BOX**
> All doctors are trained to diagnose many different diseases but the type of doctors that specialize in illnesses that affect our brains and nervous systems are called neurologists (nyur-all-lo-jists).

Tremors

When you think of Parkinson's disease, you most often think about shakiness or what we call a **tremor**. In fact this is a very common symptom and it may show up in a person's hands, arms, feet, legs, or entire body.

It's really hard to describe what a tremor feels like, but think of coming out of a swimming pool on a cool day, or being out in the snow on a really cold day without a thick enough jacket. What happens? You shiver, right? Your chin trembles and makes your teeth chatter and sometimes your whole body shakes and you can't control it. That's sort of what a tremor feels like. The good thing is that in your case, once you have a fluffy towel wrapped around you or you sip a hot cup of cocoa, you warm up and the shaking stops. Unfortunately, in Parkinson's disease it's not that simple. Warming up doesn't stop the tremors.

Bradykinesia

There are other things you might notice besides a tremor. You may think that the person in your life with Parkinson's moves very slowly when they are walking or reaching for something. It's not your imagination. They are actually moving more slowly and this is another sign of the disease called **bradykinesia** (bradi-ki-neesha). Because you are an active kid it may be hard to relate to this feeling but imagine trying to chase your friends in a swimming pool. Not by swimming, but by running along the bottom of the shallow end of the pool. You can't help but **move in slow motion** no matter how fast you want to go, right? Your legs feel heavy and the water seems to be pulling them back. Well when you have Parkinson's, it sometimes feels like that. "Sometimes you move at a snail's pace and no matter how quickly you'd like to move, it's just not possible.

Poor Balance

Now picture this. Have you ever tried to whack a piñata at a birthday party? Do you remember how you felt when your friends spun you around and around first to make it more difficult for you to know where you were and where the piñata was? And however hard you tried to keep standing in one place, you couldn't help but almost topple over? Luckily for you, that strange feeling probably passed pretty quickly. In a minute or so you felt more steady and you whacked the piñata hard enough to send the candy flying! In Parkinson's you don't need to be spun around to feel wobbly and for some people that feeling can be there most of the time. Unfortunately when your balance is bad, **sooner or later, you end up falling,** and when you're older you can really hurt yourself even with what seems like a small fall.

Rigidity

Another common problem for people with Parkinson's is stiffness in the muscles throughout the body. This is called **rigidity** (rij-i-di-tee). It's like **when you've been on a long road trip** and you first step out of the car. It may feel good to get out of the back seat but it's hard to get your legs moving for the first few steps, isn't it? That's because your legs have become stiff or rigid. Luckily for you, once you hobble around for a couple of seconds that feeling is gone and you can take off running. Well in Parkinson's when leg muscles become stiff, they stay stiff, making it hard to walk normally. This is why you see some people with Parkinson's shuffling their feet when they move.

It's not just leg muscles that get stiff, though. In fact, there can be stiffness in any muscle in the body. That's also why at times the special person in your life with Parkinson's may not have as much expression on their face. These muscles can also become stiff. Since we all look at each other's faces to see if the other person is happy, mad, or sad, it can be confusing when we don't see the

INFO BOX

Let's talk about two terms that you might hear – symptoms (sim-tums) and signs. Symptoms describe the way you feel. For instance when you have a cold, your symptoms can be a runny nose, cough, and feeling tired. A sign is something that someone else can see or measure. For example you my have a fever with your cold. Your high temperature that your mom measures with a thermometer is a sign.

smile, frown or look of surprise that we are expecting. For example you've told your best joke and Grandpa says it's really funny but he's not really smiling. What are you supposed to think? Did he like it or not? Well it's not that he doesn't think you're hilarious, it's just that his face isn't cooperating with him. His muscles are stiff and he isn't able to grin the way he used to. To understand how he feels, try this. Put both hands on your cheeks and pull back. Now while you're doing that, try to smile—not so easy is it?

These symptoms and signs are the most common ones in Parkinson's but there are many other problems as well: **trouble sleeping, problems going to the bathroom, feeling sad, losing weight,** forgetting more easily, and trouble swallowing, for example.

It's important to remember that not all of these symptoms or signs happen to every person with Parkinson's disease in the same way or at the same time. It affects everyone differently. Although most symptoms tend to get worse with time, there are many scientists around the world who are working hard to help people with Parkinson's feel better. And eventually they will find a cure!

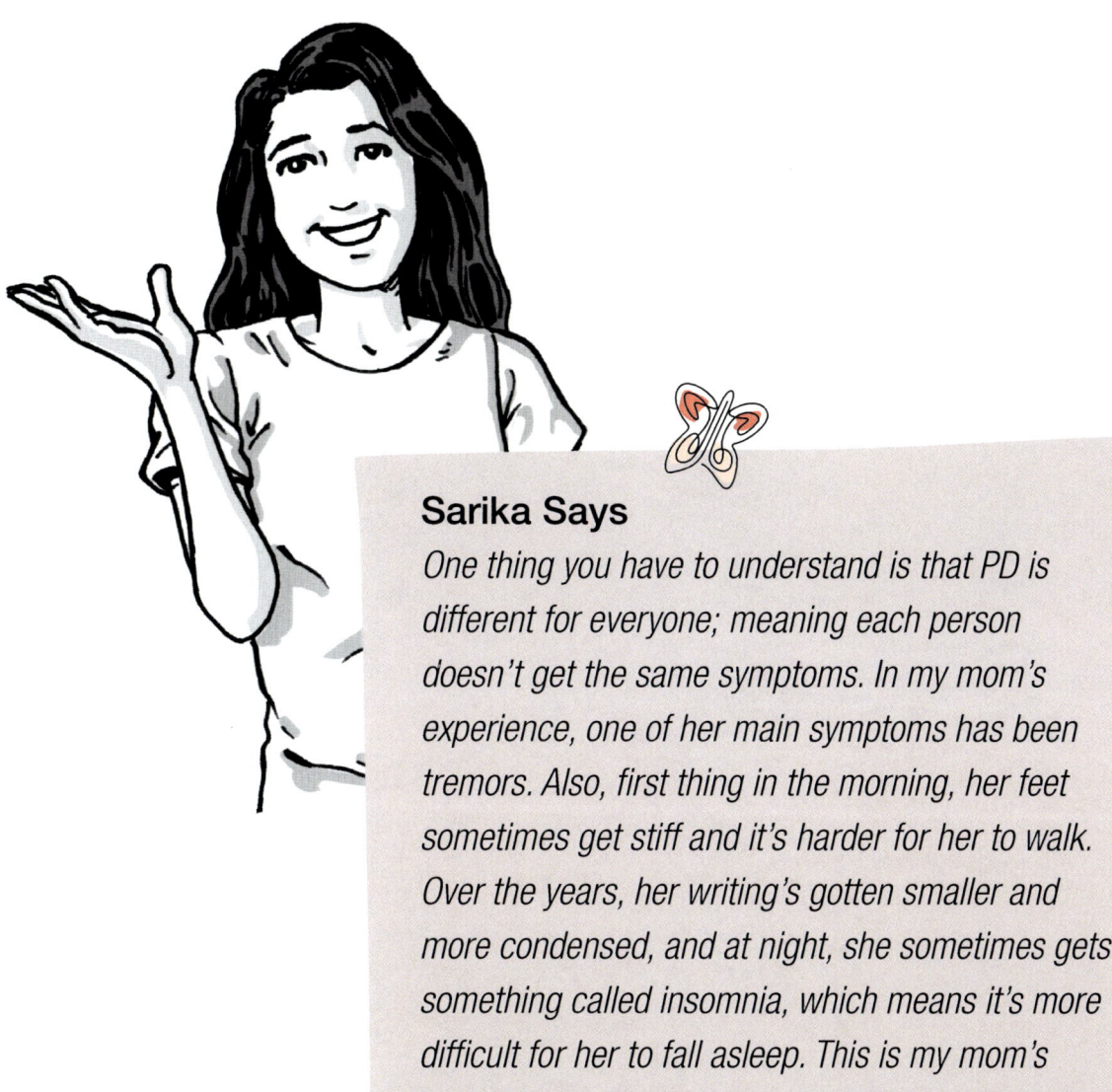

Sarika Says

One thing you have to understand is that PD is different for everyone; meaning each person doesn't get the same symptoms. In my mom's experience, one of her main symptoms has been tremors. Also, first thing in the morning, her feet sometimes get stiff and it's harder for her to walk. Over the years, her writing's gotten smaller and more condensed, and at night, she sometimes gets something called insomnia, which means it's more difficult for her to fall asleep. This is my mom's case, but the person you know may have different symptoms altogether.

3

BUT DOESN'T YOUR MEDICINE MAKE YOU FEEL BETTER?

"I see my grandma take like a hundred pills a day! And she still shakes!"

"**So** how do doctors treat Parkinson's disease?" It may seem like grandma really does take a hundred pills and sometimes that's not far from the truth! Right now there is no cure, but there are different types of medicines to help people who have Parkinson's disease feel better.

As you learned in the first part of this book, one of the problems is that people with Parkinson's don't have enough dopamine in their brains and dopamine is what signals the brain to move the body normally. Many Parkinson's medications work by replacing the missing dopamine. Sounds easy enough, but it's not. It would be great if people with Parkinson's could just take a dopamine pill and feel like they were back to normal, but **getting the correct amount of medicine is tricky** and can be different for each person. Not enough dopamine and their

> **INFO BOX**
> What are side effects exactly? They are things that happen in your body because of the medicine. For example, a common medicine that your parents may have given you if you felt like you were going to throw up can also make you sleepy. That sleepiness is a side effect of the medicine. It's pretty difficult if you think about it— you're taking something to help you feel better but possibly end up feeling worse in a different way!

symptoms are still there; too much dopamine and there can be aggravating side effects.

One of the things that can happen when you have too much dopamine is that your body makes large movements without your control. This is called **dyskinesia** (dis-kin-neshia). Imagine your shoulders rolling towards the front and back without you wanting them to. Or your ankle twisting your foot all over the place whether you want it to or not. No matter how hard you try, you just can't stop for long. It's like an alien taking over your body! And that can be uncomfortable.

A lot of the medications also have side effects even when you're not taking too much. They can make you feel sick to your stomach, or like you might faint, or they can cause swelling or puffiness in your feet. Every day, doctors and people with Parkinson's face this challenge— trying to find the right type and the correct amount of medicine that will make them feel better without causing too many side effects. This can be very difficult to do.

Sometimes when there are too many side effects or when the medications stop working very well, doctors may suggest brain surgery. This isn't for everyone but in some cases it works. You may be thinking, **"Since when is brain surgery a good**

thing?" It might seem pretty scary, but lots of people have felt much better after having an operation called **deep brain stimulation**. Remember the electrical signals we talked about in the first chapter—the ones that dopamine triggers in the nerve cells in the brain and body? In deep brain stimulation, the surgeon puts something called a stimulator in the brain. It sends out its own electrical signals to get the body moving more normally. Basically the stimulator gets around the brain problem and fires up the right neurons directly so that the body moves better. A cool thing about this surgery is that the patients are awake during part of it so that they can tell the surgeon how they are feeling. This helps the surgeon know that the stimulator is in the right spot.

As you can see, just as each person with Parkinson's has different symptoms, each patient has a different course of treatments as well. For everybody, though, **a cure would obviously be the best thing.** Many smart scientists are working very hard to find the cure and get rid of Parkinson's disease once and for all!

> **INFO BOX**
>
> There are many different kinds of medicines, some actually make you completely better (called a cure), while others just make you feel better for a little while. For example when you have a cold, you sometimes have to take medicine to get rid of your stuffy nose or a cough. The medicine doesn't make the cold go away, but it helps you feel a bit better. On the other hand, if you have an ear infection, then taking a special medicine like an antibiotic will actually make you healthy again and get rid of the infection.

4

YOU'RE STILL THE ONE I LOVE

"Ever since the Parkinson's, everything seems like it's changed. I'm worried about what's happening."

Anyone can get Parkinson's—men or women, young adult or older. So that means that those of you reading this book may have a grandma or grandpa, mom or dad, or another person you care about, who has this disease. You may not know what to think, how to react or how to feel. Or knowing that something is wrong, you may be feeling scared or overwhelmed. It's perfectly normal to have any or all of these thoughts. It's also important to know that you are not alone in how you feel. There are many kids in the same situation. Here are some of the more common concerns kids like you have.

"I don't want things to change. I love my mom just the way she is! I want her to stay the same forever!"

With Parkinson's disease, things do change. As you've read, sometimes **the disease may affect the way a person walks,** talks, looks, or moves. The grandpa who used to take you for long walks to the park may not be able to walk as far. The dad who used to give you rides on his shoulders may not be steady or strong enough to do that anymore. The grandma who used to do arts and crafts with you may not be able to hold her hand steady enough to show you new things. And the mom who used to play games with you in the backyard, may have to cheer you from the sidelines instead.

How much life will change will be different for every family. There will be better days and worse days. I know that when the person you love moves, looks, or talks differently, it can be difficult to know how to react. But remember that even though there are lots of changes happening to their bodies, they are still the same people. Who they are and what makes them a special person to you isn't different at all.

Think of it this way. A present is the same no matter how you wrap it, isn't it? Whether it's in a big box, a pretty bag, or has a fancy bow, inside the present is still the same. You will enjoy the gift no matter how it was wrapped. Having people in your life whom you care about—and who care about you—is a beautiful gift. It's just the packaging, the changes that happen in Parkinson's, that is a bit different! They are still the same people you've always loved and who've always loved you. And that is one thing that will not change.

"I'm scared about all the changes I see happening. My dad doesn't look the same and his movements are strange. But I don't want him to feel bad that I'm noticing he's different."

When you care about someone it's natural to not want to hurt their feelings. You might think that it will make them feel badly or embarrassed if you ask about the changes you have noticed. But if the changes are obvious enough for you to see, you can be sure that the person who has the disease is already aware that they aren't acting or looking the way they used to either.

If you're wondering why grandpa shuffles slowly down the hallway, ask him! If you're a bit scared by grandma's shaky hands, talk about it! If you're upset that mom or dad can't run around with you as much as before, tell them! Even though

Sarika Says

At first, you're going to be scared or nervous to talk to people about what's going on. Don't deny it, it's true. We all go through it at some point and its completely understandable, given the situation we're in. But don't be afraid! No one's going to bite. Ask questions! The only way you're going to get over your nervousness is if you understand it. Me, I just went straight to my mom. I asked everything I wanted to know. She answered almost all my questions, and helped me through it. And she's still the same person. In the two seconds before and after you found out, the person you know didn't magically change who they are. They're still the same person you know and love. Just remember that and everything will be easier. Believe me.

it may be difficult to start the conversation, it is a discussion that you need to have because **no one can help with your worries if you don't ask.** If it's too difficult to share what you're wondering about with the person who has

Parkinson's, you may want to speak with someone else that you trust—maybe a parent or grandparent, another relative, or a close family friend. You could even tag along to the next neurologist's appointment to ask about what is puzzling you. That's a great way to get the information you need. Or there are people who are experts in exploring your feelings and helping you feel better. They're called therapists, and your mom or dad can certainly make an appointment for you to see someone like this if you need to. By asking questions and sharing your feelings, not only will you feel much better, but also it will let those who care about you answer those questions openly, which makes everyone more comfortable. No one wants you to walk on eggshells; they want you to feel comfortable with what's going on.

Sarika Says

When I first found out my mom had Parkinson's disease, I was shocked. Shocked and confused. Personally, I had no idea that this had been going on so long, or even that it had been going on at all! I had no idea what this was, and you could fill a book with the number of 'Whys' I had. Why is this happening? Why did this happen to did this happen to my mom, of all people? Why hasn't anyone told me? Why didn't I figure it out? Why can't we cure it? Why, why, why, why, why.

So talk it out with them. Let them know that you're scared. **It's better to discuss your fears** than letting those thoughts grow inside you.

"I'm so confused. I just don't know about what's going to happen in the future."

It's normal to be unsure of what to expect. After all, this is completely new to you. So what can you do about it? Read, listen, and learn!

Sarika Says
I'll tell you the truth; if you've got some questions, it may be a little awkward asking them. One tip I have is to start it out with something like, "Just wondering…"; make it sound casual. It'll seriously make it easier.

Asking questions is a great way to get the information you need. Have you ever heard someone say "Knowledge is power"? Learning about Parkinson's will give you power over your fears. Once you understand why these things are happening and what to expect, the situation doesn't seem so scary.

And once you feel a little more comfortable with how your family is changing, you'll also be able to think about how you can help, which takes us to the next, and last, part of this book.

Sarika Says
What do I think about the future? That's a silly question. It's silly because the answer is obvious. Of course we're going to find a cure. Someday soon, I know it. Everything is going to get a lot better, you'll see. We just have to have faith.

5

I can make a difference!

"I want to help out
and make things better,
but what can I do?
I'm just a kid!"

Just a kid? Being a kid doesn't mean you can't help out—there's a lot that you can do! In fact, you are probably more imaginative and creative than most adults. You can make a difference in your family, in your community, and even in the world. If you're wondering how to go about doing this, I have a few suggestions.

Sometimes it's about helping the person directly. As you've read, Parkinson's symptoms can sometimes make it difficult for people to move, walk, and do things for themselves. So if you see that grandpa is having trouble getting out of his chair, help him up. If your mom's hands are shaking too much to pull the zipper up on her dress, then do it for her. If grandma seems unsteady going up the steps, hold her hand. These may seem like little things, but small actions can make big differences!

Sarika Says

One way to make your loved one feel a lot better is to help out around the house. For example, when my mom needs to take her medication, I bring her a glass of water, or in the morning when her feet are cramping, I grab her stiff shoes so she can walk. The little things mean a lot, no matter how small.

Have you heard the saying "Charity begins at home"? Basically, what it means is that **if you're going to help out, start at home.** If the one you love with Parkinson's lives with you, then lend a hand with the day-to-day stuff. It may be as simple as keeping your room clean and making sure you put your dirty socks in the laundry hamper! Or it may be that you need to help

with chores around the house. Even if the person affected doesn't live with you, you can help out when you visit, or you can make regular visits with your parents to lend a hand. You might be surprised to find out that simple things like sweeping the floor or picking up grocery bags can be difficult for a person with Parkinson's. Imagine how hard it would be to put dishes away if your hands were always shaking. So **be more aware of what's going on around you,** see what needs to be done, and do it! You'll be amazed at how much your help will be appreciated and what a difference just a little help makes. Not only does it make everyday life easier for the whole family, but it also shows how much you care.

Now, remember those scientists I mentioned before? There are many, many scientists working really hard all over the world to find better treatments and a cure for Parkinson's disease. But in order to do all that work, they need a lot of money. Research is expensive! I'm sure you've heard of "fundraising"—collecting money for different charities that help people in different ways. You've probably done this at your school—had a bake sale or car wash to raise money for a class foster child, or maybe you've collected money door-to-door to donate to a certain charity. Well in the same way, **you can raise money to donate to scientists** so that they can continue their

Sarika Says

Fundraising is a great way to get involved! I've been doing as much as I can over the last few years, ever since I found out about my mom. I know that if we don't try and help, then nothing's ever going to happen. We need to try and join the movement, be the change. Some things my sisters and I are doing are: a couple years ago I sold friendship bracelets and gave the funds to Parkinson's research; for my birthday I asked friends and family to donate money instead of presents; and every year at our school, my sisters and I hold Pennies for Parkinson's, where we ask people to collect and donate spare change from around the house, and organize activities for the students.

work. And the more they work, the sooner there will be a cure that can help people with Parkinson's all over the world!

So what can you do to fundraise? There are lots of things you can do to get people to open up their purses or wallets to help you raise money. All it takes is a little imagination. Put on an art show or a bake sale, sell friendship bracelets that you make, have a garage sale, or host a pancake breakfast. The possibilities are endless!

Another important thing you can do is to **spread the word about Parkinson's.** Some people simply don't know about this disease and if they don't know about it, then how can they help out? Hopefully you've learned a lot about Parkinson's from this book and other information you have read or heard. Once you feel like you know your stuff, then think about teaching people in your family, school, and community about what you

know and how Parkinson's affects you and those you love. Moreover, let them know what they can do to help. The more that people know about how much Parkinson's disease affects lives, the more likely they are to donate their time and money.

They might even try to make a difference themselves. And when people work together, a lot can get be accomplished!

So you see, there's so much you can do to make a real difference in the lives of people affected by Parkinson's both at home and even around the world. And I guarantee that **you'll feel great knowing how much** you—"just a kid"—were able to help.

Sarika Says

In my opinion, having a mom with Parkinson's hasn't really changed my day-to-day life. Though sometimes she may be shaky, I know she loves me so much and will always be there for me. And it doesn't really worry me either, because I believe someday very soon there will be a cure. In the meantime, all I can do is help as much as possible and also fundraise and teach other people about the disease. I know now that you can make a difference if you really try.

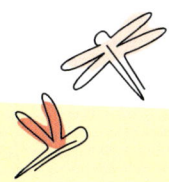

My Mom's hands shake,
And all night she stays awake.
Although she hardly gets rest,
She's still the #1 mom the best.
We go swimming, biking and more,
That way she's never a bore.
Although her hands are shaking some of the time,
She's mine and it's not a crime.
We always do stuff together,
And are always there for each other.
Although her brain is under attack,
It usually doesn't set her back.
She helps me make decisions and gives me advice,
She's a wonderful woman, sweet, kind, and nice.
I can't imagine the world without her here with me,
It would be awful, a tragedy.
She always thinks positive,
And never negative.
Above this you have to remember,
She has shaky hands but loving hands and I still love her.

—Neha

A letter from Meeraya (Age 9)

Millions of people around the world have Parkinson's but it's important to me because my mom has it. I know that it's complicated but there are scientists working very hard to find a cure. But if we get our heads together, fundraise and tell others about it, we can make a difference for my mom and everyone else who has it.

Me

Mama

Acknowledgements

First and foremost thanks to my irreplaceable husband Dr. Arun Mathur who not only stands by me through this sometimes difficult journey but is also my biggest supporter regardless of which endeavor I choose to pursue.

To my three beautiful daughters Sarika, Neha and Meeraya for their input and wisdom beyond their years. For making life worth living.

To my friend and fellow medical class graduate, Dr. Irfan Mian, Psychiatrist in the child, youth and family program at the Centre for Addiction and Mental Health in Toronto for his review and input.

To Sheba Meland and Carolyn Jackson for their time, interest and expertise. Their editing and suggestions have been invaluable.

To Salva Ferrando for his work on the illustrations.

To Barbara Leff of Monk Design Group for her dedication, hard work and creativity that went into the layout for this book.

Lastly but certainly not least, to my father Surjit Verma who instilled in me the power of educating children. He may no longer be with us but he continues to inspire me in everything that I do.

Dr. Soania Mathur is a family physician living outside of Toronto, Ontario who had to resign her practice as a result of her Young Onset Parkinson's disease a full twelve years after her diagnosis at age 27. Now she is a dedicated speaker, writer, educator and Parkinson's advocate. She speaks passionately about the challenges of adjusting physically and emotionally and the coping strategies available to patients (you can learn more about her work at **www.designingacure.com**). Dr. Mathur has a special interest in helping educate the youngest affected by the stress of this chronic disease. To help facilitate dialogue between children and their loved ones, she has authored this book as well as *"My Grandpa's Shaky Hands"*. Most importantly, she is the proud mother of three beautiful daughters and married to her loving and supportive husband Arun, a Urologic surgeon.

Made in the USA
Middletown, DE
12 May 2024

54230715R00033